Extreme Privacy

Extreme Privacy | Mastering Digital Secrecy in a Data-Driven World

GW00659432

Carl Keyness

Extreme Privacy
© Copyright 2023 by Carl Keyness
All rights reserved

This document is geared towards providing exact and reliable information with regards to the topic and issue covered. The publication is sold with the idea that the publisher is not required to render accounting, officially permitted, or otherwise, qualified services. If advice is necessary, legal or professional, a practiced individual in the profession should be ordered.

From a Declaration of Principles which was accepted and approved equally by a Committee of the American Bar Association and a Committee of Publishers and Associations.

In no way is it legal to reproduce, duplicate, or transmit any part of this document in either electronic means or in printed format. Recording of this publication is strictly prohibited and any storage of this document is not allowed unless with written permission from the publisher. All rights reserved.

The information provided herein is stated to be truthful and consistent, in that any liability, in terms of inattention or otherwise, by any usage or abuse of any policies, processes, or directions contained within is the solitary and utter responsibility of the recipient reader. Under no circumstances will any legal responsibility or blame be held against the publisher for any reparation, damages, or monetary loss due to the information herein, either directly or indirectly.

Respective authors own all copyrights not held by the publisher.

The information herein is offered for informational purposes solely, and is universal as so. The presentation of the information is without contract or any type of guarantee assurance.

The trademarks that are used are without any consent, and the publication of the trademark is without permission or backing by the trademark owner. All trademarks and brands within this book are for clarifying purposes only and are owned by the owners themselves, not affiliated with this document.

TABLE OF CONTENTS

CHAPTER 1: INTRODUCTION TO EXTREME PRIVACY

In today's hyper-connected world, where data flows freely and digital footprints accumulate with every click, the concept of privacy has become increasingly elusive. We live in an era where our online activities are constantly monitored, analyzed, and monetized by corporations and, in some cases, even governments. As we delve into the world of extreme privacy, it's essential to begin with a solid understanding of its importance, the lurking threats to our online privacy, and the delicate balance between privacy and convenience.

1.1 The Importance of Privacy in the Digital Age

Privacy is a fundamental human right that has taken on renewed significance in the digital age. It forms the cornerstone of personal freedom and autonomy, enabling individuals to control their personal information and protect themselves from unwarranted intrusion. In an era where our lives are increasingly lived online, the importance of privacy cannot be overstated.

Preserving Individual Autonomy: Privacy allows individuals to make choices without fear of judgment or coercion. It enables us to explore diverse opinions, lifestyles, and identities without undue influence.

Protecting Personal Information: Our digital lives are filled with sensitive information, from financial data to personal communications. Privacy safeguards this information from falling into the wrong hands.

Fostering Trust: Privacy is crucial for building trust in our digital interactions. When individuals trust that their personal data will be handled responsibly, they are more likely to engage in online activities and transactions.

1.2 Understanding the Threats to Online Privacy

In the digital realm, there are numerous threats to our privacy, some more subtle than others. Understanding these threats is the first step towards safeguarding our personal information.

Data Collection and Profiling: Companies routinely collect data about our online behavior, creating detailed profiles that can be used for targeted advertising or sold to third parties. This practice often occurs without our explicit consent or knowledge.

Identity Theft and Fraud: Cybercriminals are constantly seeking to exploit vulnerabilities to steal personal information and commit identity theft or financial fraud. Vigilance is essential to prevent falling victim to these crimes.

Government Surveillance: Some governments engage in mass surveillance programs, monitoring citizens' online activities. While these programs may be conducted under the guise of national security, they raise significant privacy concerns.

1.3 Navigating the Balance between Privacy and Convenience

In our quest for privacy, we must acknowledge that it can sometimes conflict with the convenience and functionality of the digital services we rely on daily. Striking the right balance is an ongoing challenge.

Privacy vs. Convenience: Many services offer convenience at the expense of privacy. Consider social media platforms that encourage sharing personal information for networking and engagement. Finding the right balance requires careful consideration of what you're willing to share.

The Role of Encryption: Encryption is a powerful tool for protecting data privacy. While it adds a layer of security to our communications, it can also be seen as an inconvenience, as it may require additional steps for secure access.

Personal Responsibility: Ultimately, the responsibility for preserving privacy lies with the individual. Being informed about privacy settings, understanding the implications of data sharing, and making conscious choices are vital steps in achieving a balance between privacy and convenience.

CHAPTER 2: DIGITAL FOOTPRINTS AND DATA TRAILS

In the interconnected realm of the internet, every online action leaves a trail—a digital footprint that, when pieced together, paints a vivid portrait of your virtual existence. Understanding the nature of digital footprints is the first step towards gaining control over your online privacy. In this chapter, we'll explore what digital footprints are, how companies and advertisers relentlessly track you, and the importance of uncovering your digital identity.

2.1 The Nature of Digital Footprints

Imagine walking through a pristine forest, leaving a trail of footprints in the soft soil. These footprints reveal your presence, direction, and perhaps even your state of mind. In the digital world, the concept is quite similar, except that instead of soil, it's data that captures your every move.

Persistent and Indelible: Digital footprints are persistent and nearly indelible marks left behind by your online activities. From the websites you visit to the searches you make, they accumulate over time.

Comprehensive in Scope: These footprints encompass a wide range of data, including your IP address, browsing history, location data, and even your social media interactions. Each contributes to a detailed profile of your online behavior.

Valuable to Various Parties: Your digital footprints are valuable to a host of entities, from advertisers seeking to target you with relevant ads to data brokers looking to sell your information to the highest bidder.

2.2 How Companies and Advertisers Track You

The digital landscape is rife with trackers, cookies, and algorithms designed to monitor your online actions. Companies and advertisers employ a plethora of techniques to gather data about you, often without your explicit consent.

Cookies and Tracking Pixels: Websites commonly deploy cookies—small text files—and tracking pixels to monitor your browsing behavior. These tools collect data on the pages you visit, the time spent on each page, and the actions you take.

Data Mining and Profiling: Your online interactions are mined for data, allowing companies to build detailed profiles about your interests, preferences, and habits. This information is then used to tailor ads specifically for you.

Social Media Tracking: Social media platforms are particularly adept at tracking your online behavior. They monitor not only your interactions on their platform but also your activities on third-party websites through social plugins.

2.3 Uncovering Your Digital Identity

Your digital identity is the amalgamation of your digital footprints—a multifaceted representation of your online persona. Uncovering this identity is a crucial step toward regaining control over your privacy.

Data Aggregation: Start by acknowledging the extent of your digital footprint. Consider the various platforms, apps, and websites you use regularly and the data they collect about you. Awareness is the first step.

Review Privacy Settings: Most online services provide privacy settings that allow you to control what information you share. Take the time to review and adjust these settings to align with your privacy preferences.

Online Audits: Conduct regular audits of your online presence. Search for your name online and assess the information that comes up. Look for outdated or inaccurate data that might need correction or removal.

As you delve deeper into the world of extreme privacy, remember that understanding your digital footprints is the foundation upon which you'll build your fortress of online anonymity. It's not about erasing your presence entirely but rather about taking control of what you share and who has access to it. In the chapters ahead, we'll explore techniques and tools that can help you minimize your digital footprint, protect your online privacy, and achieve the level of control you desire in the digital realm.

CHAPTER 3: SECURING YOUR ONLINE PRESENCE

In a world where our digital lives are increasingly entwined with our daily routines, ensuring the security of our online presence is paramount. In this chapter, we explore strategies and techniques for safeguarding your digital identity and personal information. We'll delve into the art of creating strong and unique passwords, the critical role of two-factor authentication, and practical steps to protect your social media profiles.

3.1 Creating a Strong and Unique Password Strategy

Passwords serve as the frontline defense against unauthorized access to your accounts and personal information. Yet, many people still rely on weak and easily guessable passwords. Crafting a robust password strategy is your first line of defense in the battle for online security.

The Anatomy of a Strong Password:

A strong password is one that is both complex and unique. It should ideally include a combination of:

- Uppercase and lowercase letters

- Numbers

- Symbols or special characters

- No easily guessable words or phrases

Password Managers:

Managing numerous complex passwords can be daunting. Password managers are invaluable tools that generate, store, and autofill passwords securely. They also help you avoid using the same password across multiple accounts, which is a significant security risk.

Regular Password Updates:

Even the strongest password can become compromised over time. Make it a habit to update your passwords regularly, especially for critical accounts like email and online banking.

3.2 Two-Factor Authentication and Its Role in Privacy

Two-factor authentication (2FA) is a powerful security measure that adds an extra layer of protection to your online accounts. It requires you to provide two forms of identification to verify your identity, typically something you know (your password) and something you have (a mobile device or hardware token).

Types of 2FA:

- SMS-based 2FA: A code is sent to your mobile phone via SMS, which you must enter along with your password.

- App-based 2FA: You use a dedicated authentication app like Google Authenticator or Authy to generate time-based codes.

- Hardware Token 2FA: Physical devices generate one-time codes, providing the highest level of security.

Why 2FA Matters:

Even if someone gains access to your password, they won't be able to log in without the second authentication factor. This significantly reduces the risk of unauthorized access to your accounts.

Enabling 2FA Everywhere:

Whenever possible, enable 2FA on your online accounts, including email, social media, and financial services. Most major websites and apps support 2FA, and it's a simple yet effective way to enhance your online security.

3.3 Safeguarding Your Social Media Profiles

Social media platforms are a treasure trove of personal information, making them prime targets for cybercriminals and data-hungry advertisers. Protecting your social media profiles is vital for maintaining your online privacy.

Privacy Settings:

Review and adjust the privacy settings on your social media accounts. Limit the amount of information that is visible to the public, and restrict access to personal details to only trusted friends and connections.

Be Cautious with Sharing:

Think twice before posting personal information such as your phone number, address, or travel plans. Information that you share openly can be exploited by malicious actors.

Beware of Phishing:

Phishing attacks often target social media users. Be cautious of messages or emails asking for your login credentials or personal information, and avoid clicking on suspicious links.

Chapter 4: Encryption and Secure Communication

In the pursuit of extreme privacy, one of the cornerstones is secure communication. This chapter delves into the world of encryption, exploring its types and applications, and highlights the critical role of end-to-end encryption in safeguarding your digital conversations.

4.1 Understanding Encryption and Its Types

What Is Encryption? At its core, encryption is the process of converting information into a code to prevent unauthorized access. It's like sending a secret message that only the intended recipient can decipher.

Types of Encryption:

Symmetric Encryption: In symmetric encryption, the same key is used for both encryption and decryption. It's efficient but requires a secure way to share the key.

Asymmetric Encryption: Asymmetric encryption uses a pair of keys—a public key for encryption and a private key for decryption. This ensures that the sender doesn't need to share their private key.

End-to-End Encryption (E2EE): End-to-end encryption is a specialized form of asymmetric encryption that ensures only the intended recipient can decrypt the message. Even service providers cannot access the content of E2EE-protected messages.

4.2 Securing Your Emails and Messaging Apps

Email Encryption:

- PGP (Pretty Good Privacy): PGP is a widely used email encryption method. It uses asymmetric encryption to secure email content and attachments. Both the sender and receiver need PGP keys for encryption and decryption.

- ProtonMail and Tutanota: These email providers offer end-to-end encrypted email services, making it easy for users to send secure messages without needing to set up PGP keys themselves.

Messaging Apps:

- Signal: Signal is a popular messaging app known for its strong privacy features. It uses end-to-end encryption by default for text, voice calls, and video calls.

- WhatsApp: WhatsApp also employs end-to-end encryption for text messages, voice calls, and video calls, making it a secure option for communication.

4.3 The Importance of End-to-End Encryption

Privacy and Security: End-to-end encryption ensures that only you and the intended recipient can read your messages. This is crucial for protecting sensitive information from prying eyes, whether it's personal, financial, or professional.

Protection from Service Providers: With end-to-end encryption, service providers cannot access the content of your messages, ensuring that your communications remain confidential.

Preventing Eavesdropping: Eavesdroppers, including hackers and cybercriminals, are unable to intercept and decode your messages, adding a layer of security to your digital conversations.

Trust and Transparency: Platforms that prioritize end-to-end encryption demonstrate a commitment to user privacy, fostering trust among their user base.

Challenges with End-to-End Encryption:

- Key Management: Managing encryption keys can be complex, especially in large organizations. Lost keys can result in data loss.

- Limited Functionality: End-to-end encryption may limit some functionality, such as server-side search or backup, which requires access to message content.

- User Education: Ensuring that users understand the importance of E2EE and use it correctly is essential.

Chapter 5: Privacy-Focused Search and Email Services

In the quest for extreme privacy, it's essential to scrutinize your digital interactions, starting with the tools and services you use daily. This chapter explores alternatives to traditional search engines, secure and private email providers, and strategies for customizing your digital communication to maximize privacy.

5.1 Alternatives to Traditional Search Engines

Traditional search engines like Google, while powerful, often come with privacy trade-offs. Fortunately, there are privacy-focused alternatives that respect your online anonymity.

DuckDuckGo: DuckDuckGo is a search engine that prioritizes user privacy. It doesn't track your searches or store your search history. It also offers a "bang" feature to search other websites directly.

Startpage: Startpage is another search engine that respects user privacy. It fetches Google search results but acts as an intermediary, so Google doesn't track your IP address.

Qwant: Qwant is a European search engine that emphasizes user privacy. It doesn't track users, and it's designed to protect your personal data.

5.2 Secure and Private Email Providers

Email is a primary means of communication for many, making it a critical aspect of your digital privacy journey. Consider switching to secure and private email providers.

ProtonMail: ProtonMail offers end-to-end encrypted email services. It ensures that only you and the recipient can read the contents of your emails. ProtonMail is easy to use and offers both free and paid plans.

Tutanota: Tutanota is another email provider that offers end-to-end encryption. It's known for its secure email services and user-friendly interface.

Mailbox.org: Mailbox.org is a German email provider that emphasizes privacy and security. It offers a range of features, including encrypted email, calendar, and cloud storage.

5.3   Customizing   Your   Digital Communication for Privacy

To attain extreme privacy, you must actively customize your digital communication methods to minimize data exposure and protect sensitive information.

Email Encryption: Implement end-to-end encryption for your email communications. This ensures that even if your email provider is compromised, your messages remain secure. Encourage your contacts to use encrypted email as well.

Secure Messaging Apps: Embrace messaging apps that offer end-to-end encryption by default. Signal, WhatsApp, and Telegram are examples of such apps that prioritize user privacy.

Disposable Email: Use disposable email services when signing up for online accounts or services that don't require your primary email address. This helps keep your main email address private.

Limit Data Sharing: Be cautious when sharing personal information online. Avoid oversharing on social media, and only provide essential information when signing up for websites or services.

Secure Communication Practices: Avoid discussing sensitive or personal matters in unencrypted emails or unsecured messaging apps. Use secure channels for private conversations.

Email Forwarding and Filters: Set up email forwarding and filters to automatically categorize and organize your email. This can help reduce the clutter in your inbox and improve your email management.

Educate Yourself and Others: Learn about the latest privacy threats and how to protect yourself. Educate your friends and family about privacy best practices to create a more privacy-conscious digital environment.

CHAPTER 6: PRIVACY IN THE SMART HOME

The rise of smart home devices has brought unprecedented convenience to our lives. However, this convenience often comes at the cost of privacy. In this chapter, we explore the world of privacy in the smart home, discussing the privacy implications of IoT (Internet of Things) devices, strategies to secure your smart home network, and the delicate balance between convenience and privacy within your own home.

6.1 IoT Devices and Their Privacy Implications

The Internet of Things (IoT): IoT devices are everyday objects connected to the internet, capable of collecting and transmitting data. These include smart thermostats, cameras, voice assistants, and even appliances like refrigerators and washing machines.

Privacy Concerns with IoT:

- Data Collection: IoT devices collect data about your habits, preferences, and even physical movements within your home.

- Data Sharing: Manufacturers may share this data with third parties for analysis or advertising purposes, raising concerns about the security and privacy of your information.

- Unauthorized Access: Weak security measures on IoT devices can make them vulnerable to hacking, potentially giving unauthorized individuals access to your home.

Mitigating IoT Privacy Concerns:

- Research Devices: Before purchasing an IoT device, research the manufacturer's privacy policies and security practices. Choose reputable brands with strong privacy measures.

- Change Default Settings: When setting up IoT devices, change default passwords and settings to enhance security. Enable encryption and two-factor authentication when available.

- Regular Updates: Keep your IoT devices' firmware and software up-to-date to patch security vulnerabilities.

6.2 Securing Your Smart Home Network

Secure Your Wi-Fi Network:

- Strong Passwords: Use a strong and unique password for your Wi-Fi network to prevent unauthorized access.

- Network Segmentation: Segment your network to isolate IoT devices from critical devices like computers and smartphones. This limits potential access points for hackers.

- Firewalls: Install and configure firewalls to filter incoming and outgoing traffic, adding an extra layer of security.

IoT Device Security:

- Change Default Credentials: Always change default usernames and passwords on IoT devices.

- Regularly Update: Ensure that your IoT devices receive regular software updates to patch security vulnerabilities.

- Network Monitoring: Use network monitoring tools to keep an eye on the traffic generated by your IoT devices. Any unusual activity can be a sign of a breach.

6.3 Balancing Convenience and Privacy at Home

Balancing convenience with privacy in a smart home can be a challenging task, but it's crucial for maintaining control over your digital life.

Privacy Settings: Review the privacy settings of each IoT device in your home. Disable unnecessary data collection features, limit access to data, and opt out of sharing data with third parties when possible.

Data Storage: Some smart devices store data locally, while others use cloud storage. Consider which option aligns better with your privacy preferences. Local storage gives you more control, but cloud storage offers convenience.

Voice Assistants: If you use voice assistants like Amazon Alexa or Google Assistant, be aware that they record and store your voice commands. You can review and delete these recordings periodically.

Guest Network: Consider setting up a separate guest network for IoT devices when guests visit. This prevents them from accessing your primary network and critical devices.

Regular Privacy Audits: Conduct regular privacy audits of your smart home. Review and update settings, delete unused devices, and keep track of how your data is being used.

Striking a balance between convenience and privacy in a smart home is a continuous effort. By understanding the privacy implications of IoT devices, securing your smart home network, and proactively managing the settings and data collection practices of your devices, you can enjoy the benefits of a connected home while preserving your privacy. In the chapters ahead, we'll continue to explore advanced techniques and tools to help you achieve extreme privacy in every aspect of your digital life.

CHAPTER 7: SOCIAL MEDIA AND ONLINE PRIVACY

In the age of social media, the line between personal and public life has blurred. While these platforms offer connectivity and a sense of community, they also pose significant threats to your online privacy. In this chapter, we'll explore the risks associated with social media, how to manage your privacy settings effectively, and best practices for sharing on these networks while safeguarding your extreme privacy.

7.1 Privacy Risks Associated with Social Media

Data Collection: Social media platforms thrive on collecting vast amounts of user data, including your personal information, interests, and online behavior.

Tracking: Social media networks often track your online activity, even when you're not using their services. This allows them to build detailed profiles and serve targeted ads.

Third-Party Apps: Many social media apps integrate with third-party applications, which may have access to your data. These apps can sometimes be less secure than the social media platform itself.

Privacy Breaches: Social media platforms are not immune to data breaches. A breach can expose your personal information and potentially lead to identity theft.

Cyberbullying and Harassment: Sharing personal information on social media can make you vulnerable to cyberbullying, harassment, or even stalking by malicious individuals.

7.2 Managing Your Privacy Settings

Review Privacy Policies: Start by reviewing the privacy policies of the social media platforms you use. Understand how they collect, store, and share your data.

Adjust Your Privacy Settings:

- Profile Information: Limit the amount of personal information you share on your profile. Minimize the visibility of sensitive details such as your phone number and address.

- Who Can See Your Posts: Adjust the audience for your posts. You can often choose to share content with friends only, specific groups, or the public.

- Third-Party Apps: Regularly review and revoke access to third-party apps that have access to your social media accounts.

- Location Data: Disable location tracking on your posts to prevent others from knowing your exact whereabouts.

- Timeline and Tagging: Manage who can post on your timeline and tag you in photos and posts. Consider enabling review features to approve tags before they appear.

Regular Privacy Checkups: Periodically review and update your privacy settings as social media platforms often change their policies and features.

Use Two-Factor Authentication: Enable two-factor authentication (2FA) to add an extra layer of security to your social media accounts. This makes it much harder for unauthorized users to gain access.

7.3 Best Practices for Sharing on Social Networks

Think Before You Share: Before posting anything, consider whether it's necessary to share that information. Avoid posting sensitive personal details like your home address or financial information.

Use Strong Passwords: Create strong, unique passwords for each of your social media accounts. Avoid using easily guessable information such as birthdays or names.

Be Wary of Requests: Be cautious about accepting friend requests or following unfamiliar accounts. Scammers and malicious individuals often use fake profiles to gain access to your information.

Educate Yourself and Others: Stay informed about the latest privacy threats and educate your friends and family about privacy best practices.

Regularly Audit Your Friends/Followers: Periodically review your friends or followers list. Remove or block anyone who makes you uncomfortable or is a potential security risk.

Report and Block: If you encounter harassment or suspicious behavior, report it to the platform and block the offending user.

Be Mindful of Location Services: Be aware that some social media platforms may track and share your location by default. Review your location settings and disable them when not needed to safeguard your privacy further.

Social media can be a valuable tool for communication and connection, but it comes with privacy risks that require vigilance and proactive management. By understanding these risks, adjusting your privacy settings, and adopting best practices for sharing on social networks, you can strike a balance between enjoying the benefits of social media and maintaining your extreme privacy. In the chapters that follow, we'll delve deeper into advanced privacy strategies and tools to help you further fortify your online presence.

CHAPTER 8: PROTECTING YOUR FINANCIAL PRIVACY

In the digital age, financial transactions are increasingly conducted online, and your financial data is a prime target for cybercriminals. This chapter explores strategies to safeguard your financial privacy, covering topics such as online banking security, avoiding scams and phishing attacks, and the role of cryptocurrencies in enhancing your financial privacy.

8.1 Online Banking and Financial Security

Online banking offers unparalleled convenience, but it also exposes you to various security risks.

Protecting your financial privacy begins with securing your online banking practices.

Secure Passwords:

- Use strong, unique passwords for your online banking accounts. Avoid easily guessable information like birthdays or names.

- Enable two-factor authentication (2FA) whenever possible. This adds an extra layer of security to your accounts.

Secure Your Devices:

- Ensure that the devices you use for online banking are secure. Keep your operating systems, browsers, and antivirus software up-to-date.

- Use a dedicated, secure computer for online banking to reduce the risk of malware infection.

Be Cautious of Emails and Links:

- Beware of phishing emails that impersonate your bank or financial institution. Do not click on suspicious links or download attachments from unknown sources.

- Avoid accessing your online banking through links provided in emails. Instead, type the official URL directly into your browser.

Regularly Monitor Your Accounts:

- Review your bank and credit card statements regularly for unauthorized transactions. Report any discrepancies immediately to your financial institution.

8.2 Avoiding Scams and Phishing Attacks

Scammers are constantly devising new schemes to defraud individuals of their money and sensitive information. Protecting your financial privacy involves staying vigilant and avoiding common scams and phishing attacks.

Common Scams:

- Tech Support Scams: Scammers may impersonate tech support agents and claim that your computer is infected with malware. They then ask for payment to fix the issue.

- Investment Scams: Be cautious of unsolicited investment opportunities promising high returns with little risk. Verify the legitimacy of investment offers before committing.

- Charity Scams: Fraudsters may impersonate charitable organizations during crises to solicit donations. Always verify the legitimacy of charities before donating.

Avoiding Phishing Attacks:

- Be skeptical of unsolicited emails, especially those requesting personal or financial information.

- Check the sender's email address for discrepancies or unusual characters. Legitimate organizations use official domain names.

- Hover over links to view the actual URL before clicking. Ensure it matches the organization's official website.

- If you receive an email requesting sensitive information, contact the organization directly through official channels to verify the request.

8.3 Cryptocurrencies and Their Role in Privacy

Cryptocurrencies offer a unique opportunity to enhance your financial privacy, thanks to their decentralized and pseudonymous nature.

Privacy Coins:

- Some cryptocurrencies, known as privacy coins (e.g., Monero, Zcash, and Dash), prioritize anonymity by obfuscating transaction details. Consider using these coins for added financial privacy.

Wallet Security:

- Secure your cryptocurrency wallet with strong passwords and, if available, enable two-factor authentication.

- Use hardware wallets for long-term storage of cryptocurrencies. These offline devices are less susceptible to hacking.

Private Transactions:

- Utilize cryptocurrency features that enhance privacy, such as CoinJoin or Confidential Transactions, when available.

Be Informed:

- Educate yourself about the privacy features and potential risks associated with the cryptocurrencies you use.

While cryptocurrencies can enhance your financial privacy, they also introduce risks, such as price volatility and the potential for loss of funds due to mishandling. Therefore, it's essential to strike a balance between using cryptocurrencies for privacy and exercising caution.

Protecting your financial privacy requires a combination of secure online banking practices, vigilant awareness of scams and phishing attacks, and a thoughtful approach to using cryptocurrencies. By adopting these strategies, you can safeguard your financial information and maintain control over your financial privacy in an increasingly digital financial landscape. In the upcoming chapters, we'll delve into advanced privacy techniques and tools to help you further strengthen your digital privacy in all aspects of your life.

Chapter 9: Legal and Ethical Aspects of Extreme Privacy

In the pursuit of extreme privacy, it's essential to understand the legal and ethical dimensions that surround the protection of your personal information and digital identity. This chapter explores the complex landscape of privacy laws and regulations, ethical considerations when safeguarding your privacy, and the evolving future of privacy in the digital age.

9.1 Privacy Laws and Regulations Around the World

Data Protection Laws:

- General Data Protection Regulation (GDPR): The GDPR, enforced in the European Union, sets stringent rules for the collection, processing, and storage of personal data. It grants individuals greater control over their data and requires organizations to obtain explicit consent for data processing.

- California Consumer Privacy Act (CCPA): In the United States, the CCPA provides California residents with certain privacy rights, including the right to know what personal information is being collected and the right to opt-out of the sale of their data.

- Other National Laws: Many countries have enacted their own data protection laws, such as the Personal Information Protection and Electronic Documents Act (PIPEDA) in Canada or the Personal Data Protection Act (PDPA) in Singapore.

Government Surveillance:

- Patriot Act (USA): The USA PATRIOT Act expanded the U.S. government's surveillance capabilities, raising concerns about the privacy of American citizens.

- CLOUD Act (USA): The Clarifying Lawful Overseas Use of Data (CLOUD) Act allows U.S. law enforcement to access data stored overseas, potentially impacting the privacy of individuals worldwide.

9.2 Ethical Considerations in the Pursuit of Extreme Privacy

Balancing Privacy and Security:

- Ethical considerations often revolve around the balance between individual privacy and the need for security. While privacy is a fundamental human right, governments and organizations argue that certain security measures may require the intrusion of privacy, such as surveillance to combat terrorism.

Transparency and Accountability:

- Ethical privacy practices include transparency about data collection and use. Individuals should have clear information about how their data is being used and by whom.

Consent and Control:

- Respecting individuals' consent and control over their data is crucial. Ethical practices involve obtaining explicit consent before collecting or processing personal information.

Data Minimization:

- Collecting only the data necessary for a specific purpose is an ethical principle. Organizations should avoid unnecessary data collection to minimize privacy risks.

Respect for Individuals:

- Ethical privacy practices involve treating individuals with respect and dignity, even in cases where data is collected for legitimate purposes.

9.3 The Future of Privacy in an Evolving Digital Landscape

Emerging Technologies:

- As technology evolves, new privacy challenges and opportunities arise. Emerging technologies like artificial intelligence, biometrics, and the Internet of Things will continue to impact privacy considerations.

Global Data Flow:

- With the globalization of data, individuals' personal information can easily cross international borders. The future of privacy may involve further international cooperation and agreements to protect data privacy globally.

Privacy by Design:

- Privacy by design is a concept that emphasizes integrating privacy protections into the development of technologies and systems from the outset. The future may see a greater emphasis on building privacy into the design of products and services.

Consumer Empowerment:

- The future of privacy may involve increased consumer empowerment, with individuals having greater control over their data and how it's used.

Privacy Awareness:

- As privacy concerns grow, individuals are becoming more aware of their privacy rights. This increased awareness may lead to greater demand for privacy-enhancing technologies and practices.

The legal and ethical aspects of extreme privacy are dynamic and evolving. Understanding the privacy laws and regulations that apply to your region, considering the ethical implications of your privacy choices, and staying informed about the changing landscape of privacy in the digital age are essential for anyone pursuing extreme privacy.

CHAPTER 10: PRIVACY AND ARTIFICIAL INTELLIGENCE (AI)

In a world increasingly defined by technological advancements, one of the most transformative and simultaneously challenging forces at play is Artificial Intelligence (AI). AI's pervasive presence touches nearly every aspect of our lives, offering immense benefits while raising profound concerns about our privacy. This chapter explores the intricate relationship between AI and privacy, shedding light on the impact of AI, the rise of AI-powered surveillance, and strategies to enhance privacy in this AI-driven world.

10.1 The Impact of AI on Privacy

The AI Revolution:

Artificial Intelligence has ushered in a new era of innovation and automation. From voice-activated virtual assistants to recommendation algorithms shaping our digital experiences, AI permeates our daily lives. It improves efficiency, personalization, and convenience, but this progress comes at the cost of increased data collection and analysis, challenging traditional notions of privacy.

Data-Driven Insights:

AI thrives on data. It processes vast amounts of information to learn and make predictions, raising concerns about how our personal data is collected, stored, and utilized. The more AI evolves, the greater the need for individuals to grasp the implications of AI-driven data analysis on their privacy.

The Paradox of Personalization:

AI-driven personalization is a double-edged sword. While it offers tailored experiences and recommendations, it also has the potential to create filter bubbles and echo chambers, limiting exposure to diverse perspectives. Balancing personalization with privacy is a challenge in an AI-driven world.

10.2 AI-Powered Surveillance and Privacy Concerns

Surveillance in the Digital Age:

AI has amplified surveillance capabilities, both by governments and private entities. Facial recognition, predictive policing, and social media monitoring are just a few examples of AI-powered surveillance technologies. These advancements raise significant concerns about privacy invasion and civil liberties.

The Ethics of Surveillance:

The ethical implications of AI-powered surveillance are complex. Questions about consent, bias in algorithms, and the potential for abuse demand careful consideration. Privacy advocates, policymakers, and tech companies are engaged in an ongoing debate about the responsible use of surveillance technologies.

The Right to Privacy:

The right to privacy, a fundamental human right, faces unprecedented challenges in the age of AI surveillance. Legal frameworks often struggle to keep pace with technological developments. Striking a balance between security and individual privacy is an ongoing societal challenge.

10.3 Enhancing Privacy in an AI-Driven World

Privacy by Design:

Privacy by design is a critical concept in the development of AI systems. It involves integrating privacy features into the design and architecture of AI applications from the outset. This proactive approach aims to minimize privacy risks and prioritize user data protection.

Transparency and Accountability:

To enhance privacy in an AI-driven world, transparency and accountability are essential. Users should have access to clear information about how AI systems operate and impact their privacy. Furthermore, accountability mechanisms must hold organizations responsible for data breaches or misuse of AI.

Empowering Individuals:

Empowering individuals with tools and knowledge to protect their privacy in an AI-driven world is crucial. Privacy-conscious users can utilize encryption, secure communication platforms, and privacy-focused browsers to mitigate risks.

CHAPTER 11: PRIVACY IN THE AGE OF BIOMETRICS

Biometric authentication has rapidly gained popularity as a secure and convenient method for verifying individual identities. Fingerprint scans, facial recognition, iris scans, and even voice recognition have become common features on our smartphones and in various industries. While these technologies offer unparalleled security, they also introduce unique challenges to our privacy. This chapter delves into the rise of biometric authentication, the privacy concerns it raises, and strategies for safeguarding your biometric privacy in an increasingly biometric world.

11.1 The Rise of Biometric Authentication

Biometrics: The New Frontier:

The concept of biometrics revolves around using unique physical or behavioral characteristics, such as fingerprints or facial features, to identify and authenticate individuals. Biometrics have gained immense popularity in recent years due to their reliability and convenience in a variety of applications.

Biometrics in Everyday Life:

From unlocking our smartphones and securing our financial transactions to airport security checks and healthcare access, biometric authentication has become an integral part of our daily lives. Its seamless integration offers a level of security and convenience that traditional authentication methods struggle to match.

The Appeal of Biometrics:

The appeal of biometric authentication lies in its simplicity. Remembering passwords or PINs can be challenging, and these credentials are susceptible to theft or compromise. Biometrics provide a more secure and user-friendly alternative, making them increasingly prevalent in both personal and professional spheres.

11.2 Biometric Data Privacy Challenges

The Uniqueness of Biometric Data:

Biometric data, such as fingerprints and facial features, is inherently unique to each individual. However, this uniqueness also means that once compromised, it cannot be changed. This sets biometric data apart from passwords, which can be reset or changed if compromised.

Data Security and Storage:

The security and storage of biometric data present significant challenges. When organizations collect and store biometric data, they must do so with the utmost care to prevent data breaches. A breach of biometric data can have severe and lasting consequences for individuals.

Privacy and Consent:

Obtaining informed consent for collecting and using biometric data is crucial. Users should understand how their biometric data will be used and have the option to opt out. Balancing convenience with privacy requires transparent policies and user choice.

11.3 Protecting Your Biometric Privacy

Biometric Encryption:

Biometric encryption techniques allow biometric data to be stored and processed in a secure, encrypted form. This ensures that even if the data is compromised, it remains indecipherable without the appropriate decryption keys, enhancing privacy and security.

Two-Factor Authentication (2FA) with Biometrics:

Combining biometric authentication with traditional methods like PINs or passwords provides an additional layer of security. This two-factor authentication (2FA) approach ensures that even if your biometric data is compromised, an additional factor is required for access.

Know Your Rights:

Understanding your rights regarding biometric data is crucial. Familiarize yourself with privacy laws and regulations in your jurisdiction, and exercise your right to consent and opt out of biometric data collection when possible. Be aware of how organizations handle your biometric data and choose services and applications that prioritize privacy.

As biometric authentication becomes increasingly prevalent, it is essential to navigate the challenges it presents to our privacy proactively. Understanding the rise of biometrics, recognizing the privacy challenges they introduce, and adopting strategies to protect your biometric privacy will empower you to embrace the benefits of biometric authentication while preserving your personal privacy in an age where your unique attributes are the key to access.

Regularly Review and Update Biometric Data:

Incorporate the practice of regularly reviewing and updating your stored biometric data with service providers or organizations. By keeping your biometric information current, you can minimize the risk of using outdated data that might be less secure and better control who has access to it.

Chapter 12: Extreme Privacy for Activists and Journalists

In a world where information is power, activists and journalists play pivotal roles in shaping public opinion, holding institutions accountable, and driving social change. However, their work often puts them in the crosshairs of powerful entities, leading to increased scrutiny and digital threats. This chapter explores the critical role of privacy in activism and journalism, the digital threats faced by these individuals, and the tools and tactics they can employ to achieve extreme privacy in high-risk environments.

12.1 The Role of Privacy in Activism and Journalism

Privacy as a Shield:

Privacy is not a luxury for activists and journalists; it is a shield that protects them from unwarranted surveillance and potential harm. It enables them to conduct investigations, gather sensitive information, and communicate with sources securely.

Importance of Source Protection:

One of the cornerstones of journalism and activism is protecting sources. Whistleblowers, informants, and insiders often risk their safety to expose wrongdoing. Privacy is paramount in establishing trust and ensuring the safety of these sources.

Preserving Independence:

Privacy safeguards the independence of activists and journalists. It allows them to work free from interference, whether from government authorities, corporate interests, or other entities with vested interests in silencing dissent.

12.2 Digital Threats Faced by Activists and Journalists

Surveillance and Targeting:

Activists and journalists are prime targets for digital surveillance. Governments and malicious actors may monitor their communications, track their movements, and infiltrate their networks to gather intelligence or disrupt their activities.

Cyberattacks and Hacking:

Cyberattacks, including phishing, malware infections, and distributed denial-of-service (DDoS) attacks, are common tactics used against activists and journalists. These attacks aim to compromise their digital security, steal sensitive data, or silence their voices.

Online Harassment and Doxxing:

Online harassment, doxxing (revealing personal information online), and smear campaigns are tactics used to intimidate and discredit activists and journalists. Such attacks can have a chilling effect on their work and personal lives.

12.3 Tools and Tactics for Extreme Privacy in High-Risk Environments

End-to-End Encryption:

End-to-end encryption is a powerful tool for securing communications. Messaging apps like Signal and encrypted email services offer activists and journalists a means to communicate privately, ensuring that only intended recipients can decipher their messages.

Secure Browsing and VPNs:

Utilizing privacy-focused browsers and Virtual Private Networks (VPNs) helps mask online activity. Activists and journalists can protect their identity and location, preventing potential adversaries from tracking them online.

Secure File Storage and Sharing:

Cloud storage services with strong encryption, such as Tresorit and SpiderOak, enable secure storage and sharing of sensitive documents. These services ensure that even if data is compromised, it remains protected.

Digital Security Training:

Education is key. Activists and journalists should receive training in digital security best practices. This includes recognizing phishing attempts, securing devices, and practicing safe online behavior.

Legal Support and Advocacy:

Legal support and advocacy organizations, such as the Committee to Protect Journalists (CPJ) and the Electronic Frontier Foundation (EFF), can offer assistance and resources to individuals facing digital threats. They advocate for legal protections and work to raise awareness about the importance of digital privacy.

In an era where the pursuit of truth and social justice can lead to threats and challenges, extreme privacy is not a luxury but a necessity for activists and journalists. By recognizing the role of privacy in their work, understanding the digital threats they face, and employing tools and tactics designed for high-risk environments, these individuals can continue to shine a light on injustice and effect meaningful change while safeguarding their own safety and the privacy of their sources.

Conclusion: Embracing Extreme Privacy in the Digital Age

In the ever-evolving landscape of the digital age, the pursuit of privacy has become paramount. The journey we've undertaken through the chapters of "Extreme Privacy" has been a comprehensive exploration of the intricacies, challenges, and strategies inherent in safeguarding our most fundamental right in the digital realm.

From the very beginning, we recognized that privacy is not a luxury but a cornerstone of personal autonomy. Our voyage commenced with an understanding of its paramount importance, particularly in a world where personal data has become a coveted commodity.

We navigated the multifaceted threats to our online privacy, uncovering the intricate web of digital footprints, data trails, and surveillance mechanisms that pervade our interconnected lives. In this exploration, we acknowledged the delicate equilibrium between the conveniences of the digital world and the need to preserve our personal space.

As we delved deeper, we unveiled the power of encryption, secure communication, and privacy-focused tools to fortify our digital existence. We recognized that our online privacy is not just a passive right but an active responsibility—one that requires constant vigilance and the adoption of practical measures.

Venturing into specific domains, we explored privacy in the smart home, on social media, and in financial transactions. We navigated the complex interplay of laws and ethics surrounding privacy, emphasizing the global significance of privacy regulations and the ethical choices we make in our digital interactions.

Our journey reached its zenith in the chapters dedicated to activists and journalists, individuals whose roles are pivotal in shaping societies and safeguarding truth. We armed them with knowledge, tools, and tactics to protect their privacy and the integrity of their work in high-risk environments.

In conclusion, our voyage through "Extreme Privacy" has underscored a crucial truth: privacy is not a retreat from the digital world but an embrace of it on our terms. It is a declaration of our right to control our data, demand transparency, and harness technology as a force for good while preserving our inherent right to privacy.

As we bid farewell to this journey, let us carry forth the knowledge, tools, and commitment to navigate the realm of extreme privacy. Let us ensure that our digital existence aligns with our core principles and aspirations: autonomy, security, and the unwavering pursuit of truth and freedom in a digital age where privacy remains our most valued treasure.

Milton Keynes UK
Ingram Content Group UK Ltd.
UKHW020624041124
2557UKWH00027B/107

9 781088 081822